D1256988

dabblelab
Drawing Fun with Scooby-Doo!

DRAWING THE MYSTERY INC. GANG
with SCOOBY-DOO!

by Steve Korté

illustrated by Scott Jeralds

CAPSTONE PRESS
a capstone imprint

Published by Capstone Press, an imprint of Capstone.
1710 Roe Crest Drive
North Mankato, Minnesota 56003
capstonepub.com

Library of Congress Cataloging-in-Publication Data
Names: Korté, Steven, author. | Jeralds, Scott, illustrator.
Title: Drawing the Mystery Inc. gang with Scooby-Doo! / by Steve Korté ;
illustrated by Scott Jeralds.
Description: North Mankato, Minnesota : Capstone Press, [2022] | Series: Drawing fun with
Scooby-Doo! | Includes bibliographical references. | Audience: Ages 8–11 | Audience: Grades
4–6 | Summary: "Unmask the mystery behind drawing Scooby-Doo and his friends! With
step-by-step instructions, you'll sketch Fred, Daphne, Velma, Shaggy, Scooby, and so
much more! Best of all, drawing these classic characters has never been more fun
and easy!"—Provided by publisher.
Identifiers: LCCN 2021030708 | ISBN 9781663958884 (hardcover)
Subjects: LCSH: Cartoon characters in art—Juvenile literature. | Drawing—Technique—
Juvenile literature. | Scooby-Doo (Fictitious character)—Juvenile literature
Classification: LCC NC1764 .K67 2022 | DDC 741.5/1—dc23
LC record available at https://lccn.loc.gov/2021030708

Editorial Credits
Christopher Harbo, Editor; Tracy Davies, Designer;
Katy LaVigne, Pre-Media Specialist

Design Elements
Shutterstock: BNP Design Studio, Ori Artiste, sidmay

Printed and bound in the USA.   4608

TABLE OF CONTENTS

LET'S DRAW THE MYSTERY INC. GANG WITH SCOOBY-DOO!

BEEP! BEEP! BEEP!

The sound of a triple-level mystery alert echoes inside the Mystery Inc. headquarters.

Fred Jones rushes to a computer to check out the alert. Velma Dinkley and Daphne Blake quickly join him. Over by the fireplace, Shaggy Rogers and his canine pal, Scooby-Doo, are sharing a big bowl of Scooby Snacks.

"Scooby Snacks are the best!" declares Shaggy, as he tosses a tasty treat in the air and then catches it in his mouth.

CHOMP!

"Ruh-huh!" Scooby says, before he buries his nose in the bowl to gobble up more snacks.

"Okay, gang, we just received a report of a house being haunted at the edge of town," says Fred. "Let's go see if we can grab this ghost!"

Shaggy and Scooby both gulp nervously.

"Like, uh-oh!" says Shaggy.

"Rike, ruh-roh," agrees Scooby.

Over the years, Mystery Inc. has solved mysteries and battled creepy creatures around the world. Now it's time for you to draw the gang and their friends!

WHAT YOU'LL NEED

You are about to draw the most famous mystery-solving team in the world! But you'll need some basic tools to sketch them. Gather the following supplies before starting your awesome art.

paper

You can get special drawing paper from art supply and hobby stores. But any type of blank, unlined paper will work fine.

pencils

Drawings should always be done in pencil first. Even the pros use them. If you make a mistake, it'll be easy to erase and redo it. Keep plenty of these essential drawing tools on hand.

pencil sharpener

To make clean lines, you need to keep your pencils sharp. Get a good pencil sharpener. You'll use it a lot.

erasers

As you draw, you're sure to make mistakes. Erasers give artists the power to turn back time and undo those mistakes. Get some high-quality rubber or kneaded erasers. They'll last a lot longer than pencil erasers.

black marker pens

When your drawing is ready, trace over the final lines with a black marker pen. The black lines will help make your characters stand out on the page.

colored pens and markers

Ready to finish your masterpiece? Bring your characters to life and give them some color with colored pencils or markers.

Scooby-Doo

Scooby-Doo is the only canine member of Mystery Inc. Named Scoobert at birth, this cowardly Great Dane loves to scarf down Scooby Snacks, but he's not a big fan of cornering creepy creatures. When faced with a mysterious monster or gruesome ghoul, Scooby will cry, "Ruh-roh!" and look for a quick exit.

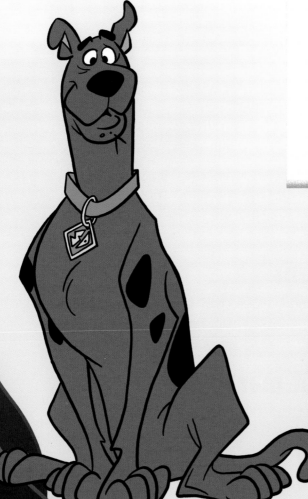

1

dRawing idea

Draw a tasty triple-decker sandwich next to Scooby.

2

3

4

5

Shaggy

1

Norville "Shaggy" Rogers is Scooby-Doo's very best friend. The two are rarely apart and often leap into each other's arms when something scares them. Shaggy also tends to goof off, and he is almost always hungry. When he's not tracking down monsters, Shaggy is usually on the hunt for a tasty snack, such as a cheese pizza with pickles.

2

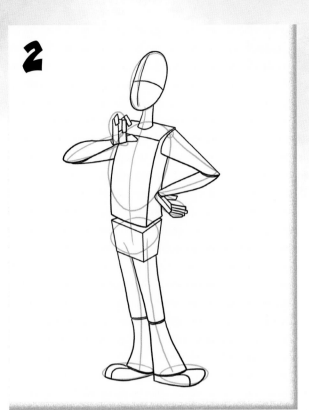

3

4

5

Daphne

1

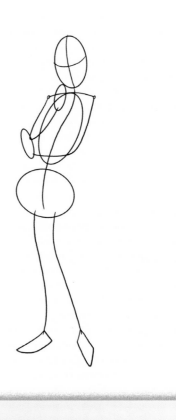

Daphne Blake's skills as an investigator stem from her background as a journalist. While nothing makes her happier than solving a good mystery, she also has a knack for getting into trouble. It's no wonder her nickname is Danger-Prone Daphne! While battling ghosts, ghouls, and other creepy creatures, it's not uncommon to hear her cry, "Jeepers!"

2

3

4

5

Fred

Fred Jones, Jr. is the unofficial leader of the Mystery Inc. gang. He is athletic, brave, and very well dressed—pretty much the opposite of Shaggy. Fred usually drives the Mystery Machine, and he is the most likely member of the team to declare, "Hey gang! It looks like we have a mystery to solve!"

1

dRawing idea
The next time you draw Fred, show him next to the Mystery Machine.

2

3

4

5

Velma

Velma Dinkley is the youngest and the smartest member of Mystery Inc. When there are creatures to catch or monsters to unmask, Velma uses her brilliant brain to follow the clues and save the day. Just about the only thing that can stop her is if she loses her glasses, causing her to say, "Jinkies! I can't see a thing without my glasses!"

1

dRawing idea

The next time you draw Velma, show her pulling a sheet off someone dressed as a ghost.

2

3

4

5

15

The Mystery Machine

1

How does the Mystery Inc. gang travel from one mystery to another? In their ultra-groovy Mystery Machine, of course! This super-cool van serves as the team's mobile headquarters and comes with a high-tech computer, a three-person scooter, and several boxes of Scooby Snacks for Shaggy and Scooby.

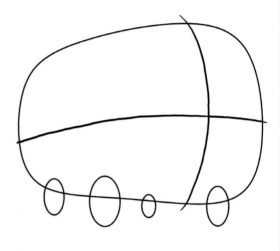

2

3

4

5

Scrappy-Doo

He's only five years old, but the pint-sized Scrappy-Doo has a lot of "puppy power!" He's Scooby-Doo's nephew, and—unlike his uncle—is one courageous canine. In fact, Scrappy sometimes leaps into action before he thinks, which can cause trouble.

1

dRawing idea

Draw Scooby-Doo next to Scrappy-Doo. Scooby is four times bigger than Scrappy!

2

3

4

5

Scooby-Dum

Scooby-Dum is Scooby-Doo's not-so-smart cousin. He lives in the Hokefenokee Swamp with restaurant owners, Ma and Pa Skillet. Although he often hinders Scooby and the gang more than he helps them, Scooby-Dum's kind and earnest nature is hard to resist.

1

dRawing idea

Add a spooky swamp background behind Scooby-Dum.

Yabba-Doo

Way out West, Scooby-Doo has a crime-fighting canine brother named Yabba-Doo. Yabba is owned by Deputy Dusty in Tumbleweed County. Unlike Scooby, Yabba is confident and courageous. But he does share his brother's love of food, especially big bowls of Chili Snacks. His favorite phrase is "Yippity-Yabbity-Doo!"

1

dRawing idea
Add a big bowl of chili next to Yabba-Doo.

2

3

4

5

Scooby-Dee

Scooby-Dee is Scooby-Doo's cousin. She is also a famous movie star. By batting her eyes and wagging her tail, she can get other canines—and quite a few people—to do whatever she wants. Her fans from all around the world just love it when she says, "Fiddle dee dee!"

1

drawing idea

Show Scooby-Dee on a movie set. Add a movie camera and a director.

Monster Truck Mystery Machine

When Shaggy wins a trip to a tropical island, he brings the Mystery Inc. team with him. It turns out that the island is really the setting for a new zombie movie, and the gang has been tricked into making an appearance in the film. Even more remarkable is a deluxe Monster Truck version of the Mystery Machine driven by Fred's stunt double!

1

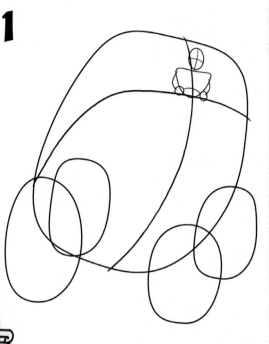

dRawing idea

Add a hairy zombie monster standing on top of the Monster Truck Mystery Machine.

2

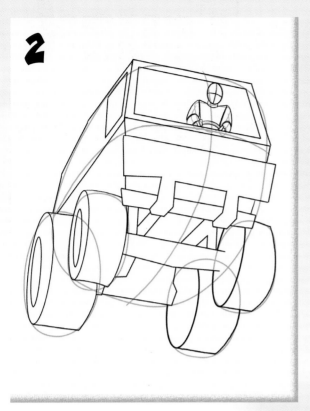

3

4

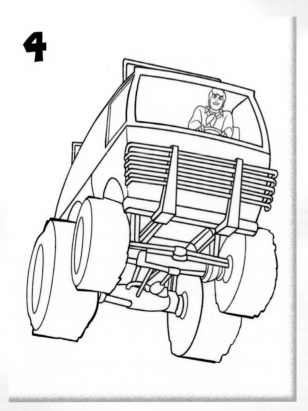

5

On the Case!

It's a dark, gloomy night in a very creepy forest. The moon is barely shining, and the Mystery Machine rolls slowly down a shadowy road in the forest. Shaggy and Scooby shiver as they peer out the window.

"Like, do you guys see those glowing eyes in the forest?" Shaggy asks.

Fred hits the brakes on the van and turns to his teammates. "Let's go, gang," he says. "We've got a mystery to solve!"

2

3

4

5

MORE DRAWING FUN!

Bird, Benjamin. *Vehicle Doodles with Scooby-Doo!* North Mankato, MN: Capstone Press, 2017.

Harbo, Christopher. *10-Minute Drawing Projects.* North Mankato, MN: Capstone Press, 2020.

Sautter, Aaron. *How to Draw Wonder Woman, Green Lantern, and Other DC Super Heroes.* North Mankato, MN: Capstone Press, 2015.

MORE SCOOBY-DOO FUN!

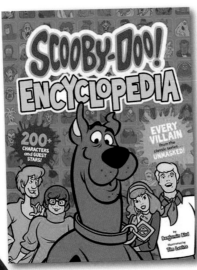

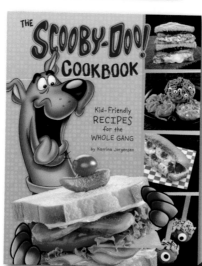

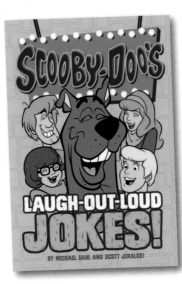